ANIMAL
FOOD

First edition for the United States, Canada,
and the Philippines published 1992
by Barron's Educational Series, Inc.

© Copyright by Aladdin Books, Ltd 1992

Design David West Children's Book Design
Illustrations Kate Taylor
Text Anita Ganeri
Picture research Emma Krikler

Created and designed by
N.W. Books
28 Percy Street
London W1P 9FF

All inquiries should be addressed to:
Barron's Educational Series, Inc.
250 Wireless Boulevard
Hauppauge, NY 11788

International Standard Book No. 0-8120-6302-3

Library of Congress Catalog Card No. 91-31325

Library of Congress Cataloging-in-Publication Data

Ganeri, Anita
Animal food / by Anita Ganeri : illustrated by Kate Taylor--1st ed.
p.   cm -- (Questions and answers about--)
Summary: Describes, in question and answer format,
some of the ways animals find food and some of the strange things they eat.
ISBN 0-8120-6302-3
1. Animals -- Food--Miscellanea--Juvenile literature. (1. Animals-
-Food habits-- Miscellanea. 2. Questions and answers.) I. Taylor,
Kate, ill. II. Title. III. Series.
QL756.5.G36   1992
591.53 -- dc20   91-31325   CIP   AC

Printed in Belgium

2345   0987654321

QUESTIONS AND ANSWERS ABOUT

ANIMAL
FOOD

Barron's

What do animals eat?

Animals need lots of food to give them energy. They spend most of their time looking for food… and avoiding being eaten themselves! Some animals eat only meat. Others are vegetarians. Others eat almost anything. Many have special features to help them reach and catch their food. This book tells you about some of the ways animals find food and about some of the strange things they eat.

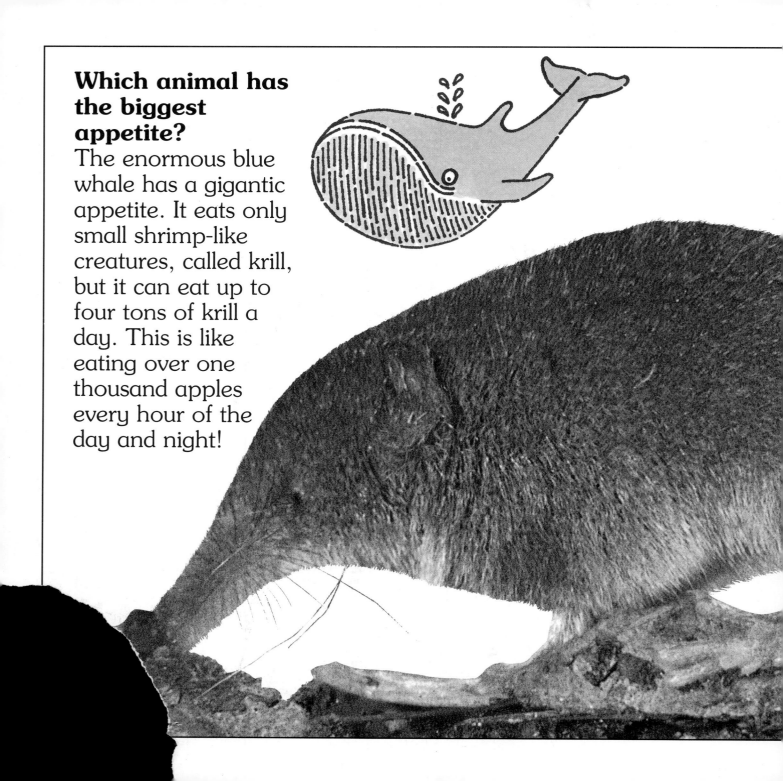

Which animal has the biggest appetite?

The enormous blue whale has a gigantic appetite. It eats only small shrimp-like creatures, called krill, but it can eat up to four tons of krill a day. This is like eating over one thousand apples every hour of the day and night!

Which is one of the hungriest animals?

The tiny pygmy shrew is *always* hungry. It eats day and night. An adult shrew only weighs about as much as a Ping-Pong ball but it eats more than its own weight every day. The shrew would starve to death if it went without food for just three hours.

Which animals squeeze their prey to death?

Boa constrictors and pythons wrap their coils around their prey and squeeze it to death. Then they swallow it whole, head first. These snakes can open their jaws wide enough to swallow antelope.

How long can snakes go without food?

Snakes can go without food for a very long time. In an experiment, a pit viper ate nothing for 3 years. It lost weight, but grew longer!

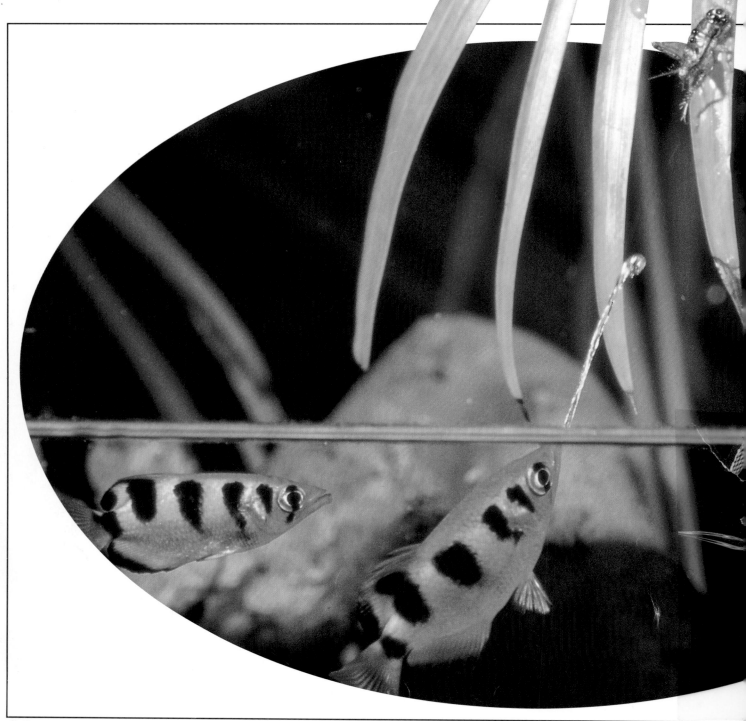

Which fish shoots its food?

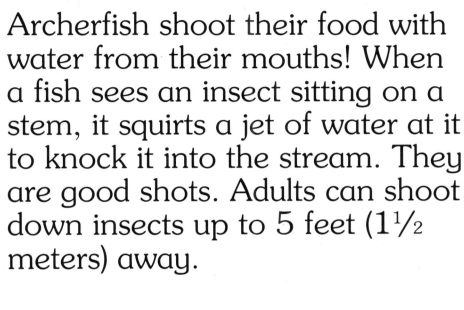

Archerfish shoot their food with water from their mouths! When a fish sees an insect sitting on a stem, it squirts a jet of water at it to knock it into the stream. They are good shots. Adults can shoot down insects up to 5 feet (1½ meters) away.

Which animals trap their food in nets?

Many spiders build silk webs to trap insects to eat. A web might look delicate, but the silk can be extremely strong. It is covered with sticky glue, so the insects cannot escape.

Which animals are not good to eat?

If an animal is brightly-colored, it usually means it is not good to eat. Animals with red and black, yellow and black, blue or white markings, may be poisonous or they sting.

Which animal smells like its food?

Koalas are very fussy about their food. They will only eat eucalyptus leaves, and only from 30 out of 500 types of eucalyptus trees. Koalas eat so much eucalyptus, that they often smell like it.

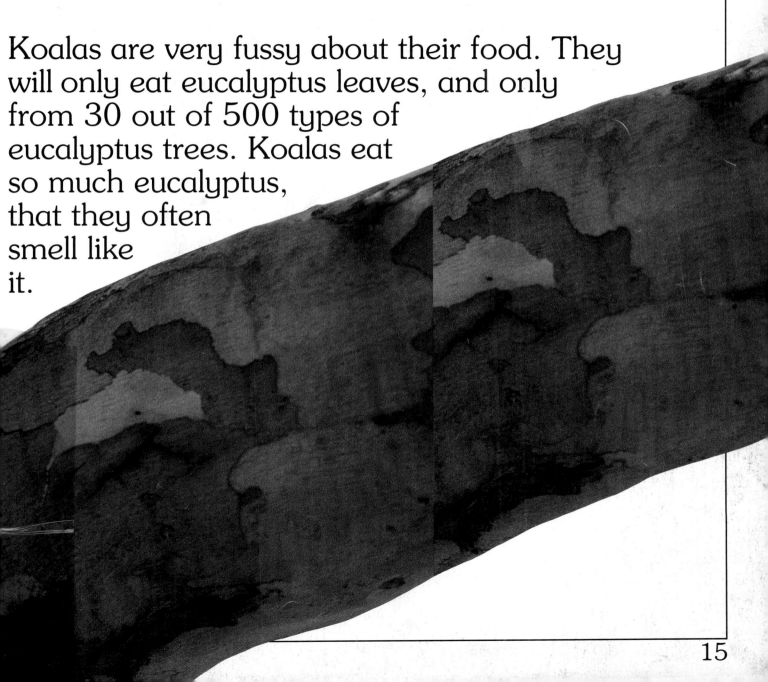

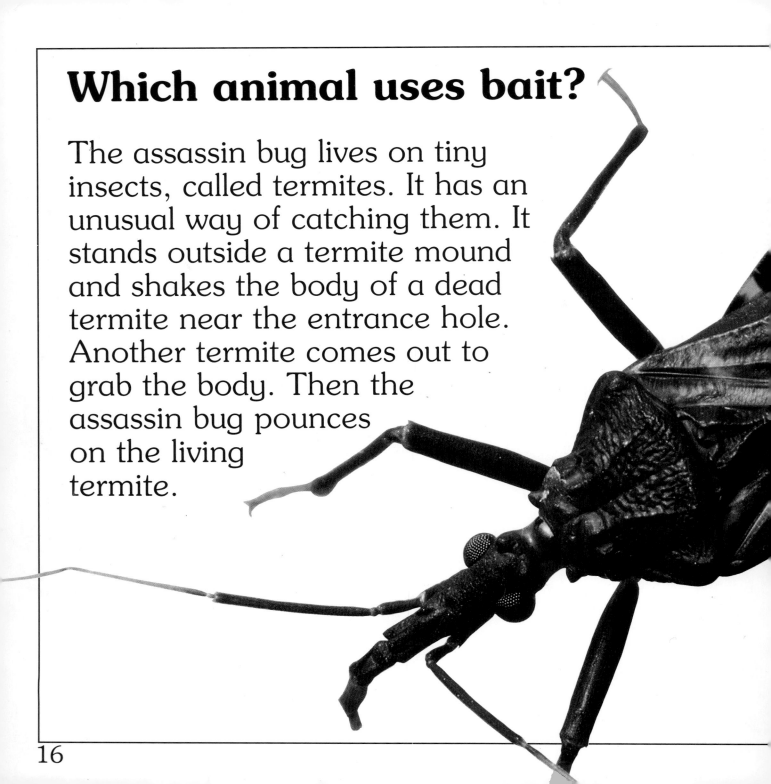

Which animal uses bait?

The assassin bug lives on tiny insects, called termites. It has an unusual way of catching them. It stands outside a termite mound and shakes the body of a dead termite near the entrance hole. Another termite comes out to grab the body. Then the assassin bug pounces on the living termite.

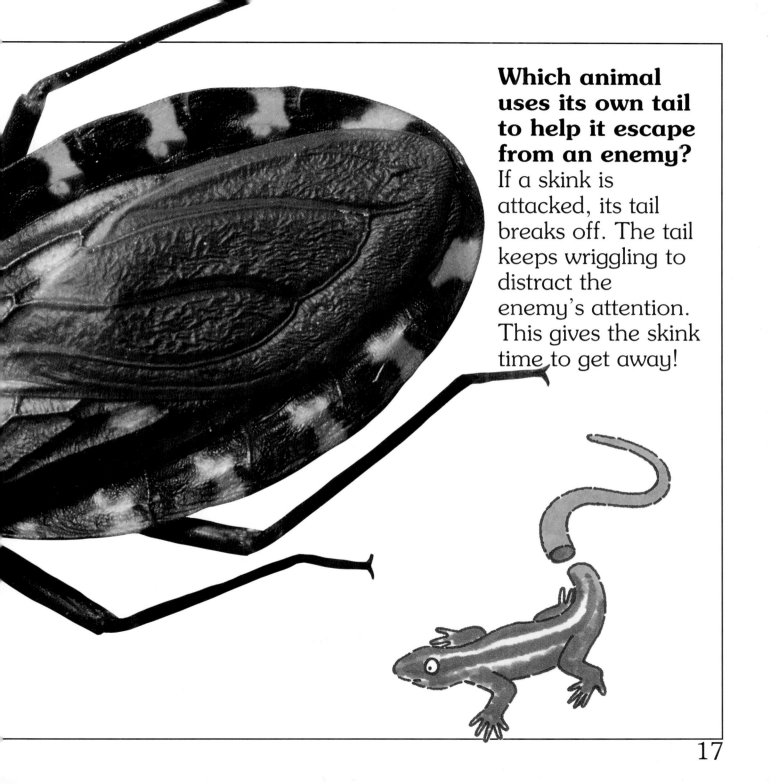

Which animal uses its own tail to help it escape from an enemy? If a skink is attacked, its tail breaks off. The tail keeps wriggling to distract the enemy's attention. This gives the skink time to get away!

17

Which animals eat blood?

Vampire bats are famous for drinking blood. Their victims are usually cows or birds which they attack at night, when they are asleep. Some vampire bats drink about a tablespoon of blood a night. Leeches and mosquitoes also eat blood. A mosquito can drink its own weight in blood every time it bites you!

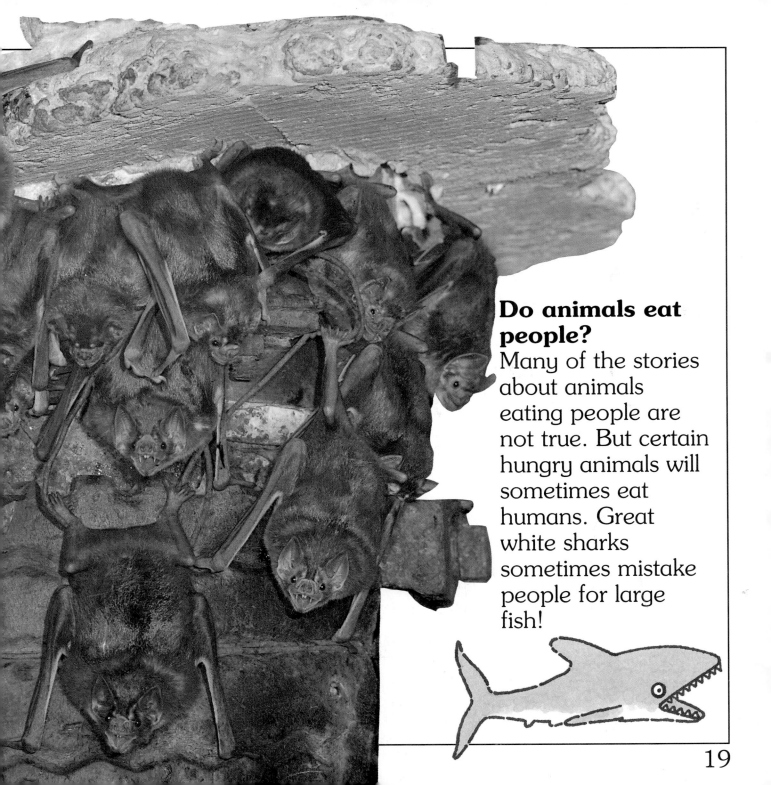

Do animals eat people?

Many of the stories about animals eating people are not true. But certain hungry animals will sometimes eat humans. Great white sharks sometimes mistake people for large fish!

Which animal seems to eat with its nose?

The giant anteater has a very long snout with a very long, sticky tongue inside it. It eats over 20,000 ants and termites a day. To find them, it breaks open an anthill with its paws and pokes its snout inside. Then it flicks its tongue in and out. It can catch about 500 ants with one lick!

Which animal has the biggest teeth?

An elephant's tusks are two of its upper teeth. Some tusks grow to be over 11 feet (more than 3⅓ meters) long.

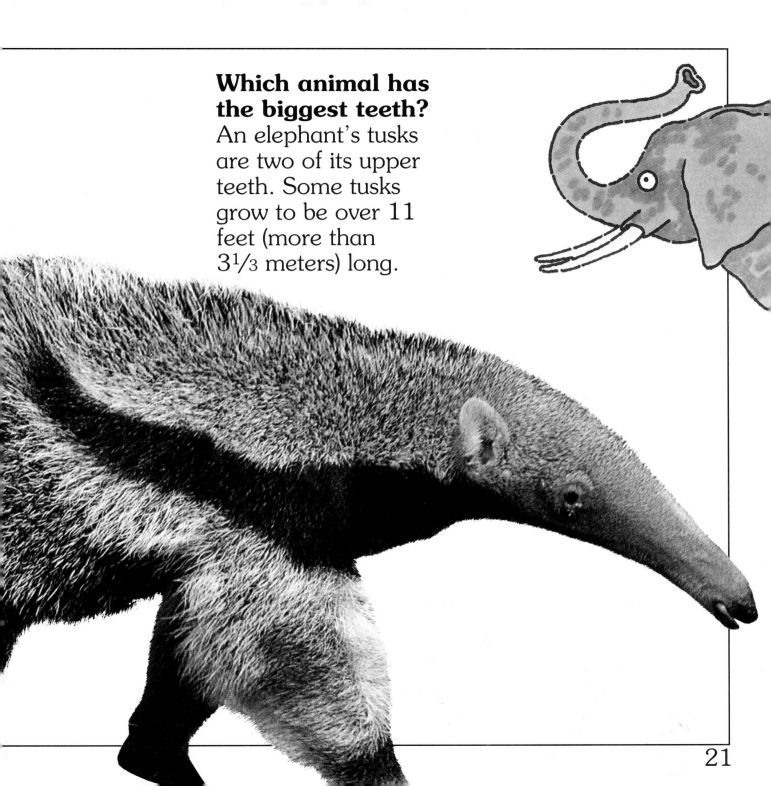

Which animals put salt on their food?

Some scientists in Japan fed sweet potatoes to a group of macaque monkeys. First, the macaques washed their potatoes in a pool. Then they discovered that washing them in the salty sea gave them a better flavor.

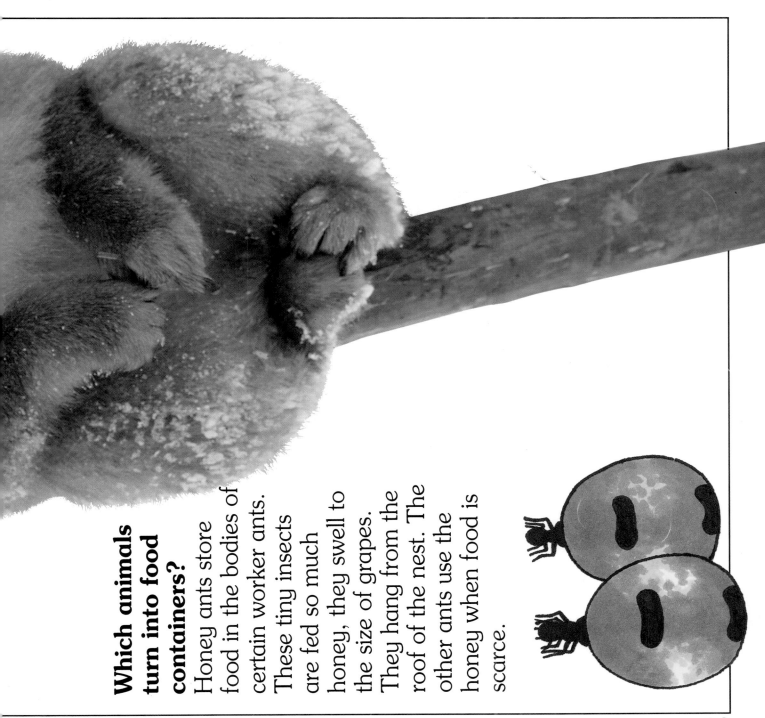

Which animals turn into food containers?

Honey ants store food in the bodies of certain worker ants. These tiny insects are fed so much honey, they swell to the size of grapes. They hang from the roof of the nest. The other ants use the honey when food is scarce.

23

Which animals use forks?

Chimpanzees eat termites from a stick just as you eat food from your fork. They peel the bark from a stick and poke it into a termite mound. When they pull the stick out, it is covered with tasty termites for them to eat. Chimpanzees have also learned to soak leaves in water and squeeze them like a sponge when they need a drink.

Which animal uses a nutcracker?
To open up a mussel to eat, a sea otter lies on its back with a stone balanced on its stomach. Then it bashes the mussel on the stone until the shell breaks open.

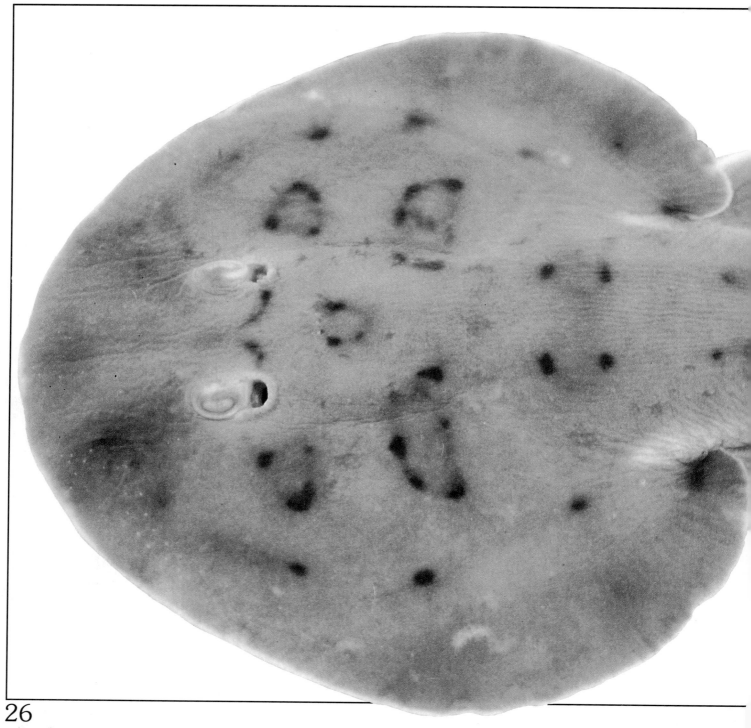

26

Which animals steal food from others?

Arctic skuas steal their food! Skuas are speedy fliers. They chase other birds and force them to drop their fish. Then they catch the fish in midair.

Which animal kills its food with an electric shock?

Electric rays catch fish by stunning them with an electric shock. They also use electric shocks to defend themselves from enemies. The biggest electric rays grow over 6 feet (2 meters) long.

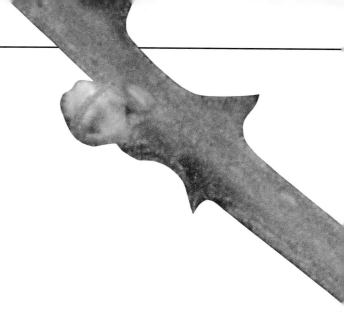

Which animals swallow pebbles?

Many birds swallow pebbles or grit to help them grind down the seeds they eat. But some swallow much stranger things. An ostrich was found to have swallowed pencils, combs, and coins.

Which animals eat wood?

Woodborer beetle grubs live inside wood, often in the furniture of people's homes. They may spend several years eating the wood and growing into adult beetles. Wood that has been attacked by woodborers has tiny holes in it. The adults leave the wood through these holes.

Index

Photographs

Cover and pages 10-11 and 26-27: Planet Earth Pictures; pages 5, 6, 8-9, 12-13, 16-17, 18-19, 20-21, 22-23, 24 and 28-29: Bruce Coleman Limited; pages 14-15: Survival Anglia Photo Library.